World At Risk

REDUCING THE CARBON FOOTPRINT

Anne Rooney

FRANKLIN WATTS
LONDON•SYDNEY

An Appleseed Editions book

First published in 2009 by Franklin Watts

Franklin Watts
338 Euston Road, London NW1 3BH

Franklin Watts Australia
Level 17/207 Kent St, Sydney, NSW 2000

© 2009 Appleseed Editions

Appleseed Editions Ltd
Well House, Friars Hill, Guestling, East Sussex TN35 4ET

Created by Q2AMedia
Editor: Katie Dicker
Art Director: Rahul Dhiman
Designers: Harleen Mehta, Ritu Chopra
Picture Researcher: Dimple Bhorwal, Shreya Sharma
Line Artist: Sibi N. Devasia
Colouring Artist: Aadil Ahmad
Technical Artists: Abhideep Jha, Bibin Jose, Manoj Joshi

ISBN 978 0 7496 8809 7

Dewey classification: 333.7

Anne Rooney asserts her right to be identified as the author of this work under the Copyright, Designs and Patent Act, 1988

All words in **bold** can be found in the glossary on pages 42–43.

Website information is correct at time of going to press. However, the publishers cannot
accept liability for any information or links found on third-party websites.

A CIP catalogue for this book is available from the British Library.

Picture credits
t=top b=bottom c=centre l=left r=right
Cover Images:Sutterstock: bg, Inset: Mark Atkins/Shutterstock: cl, Ulrike Hammerich/Shutterstock: c, Laurence Gough/Shutterstock: cr.

Laurence Gough/Shutterstock: Title Page, Sergieiev/Shutterstock: Content Page, Cinoby/iStockphoto: 9, Pascal Rateau/Shutterstock: 11,
Chelmodeev Alexander Vasilyevich/Shutterstock: 13, one clear vision/ iStockphoto: 14, Mityukhin Oleg Petrovich/Shutterstock: 15,
Arctic Images /Alamy: 16, Richard Vogal/Associated Press: 17, Pilar Echevarria/ Shutterstock: 18, Linde/ iStockphoto: 19,
Teb Nad/Shutterstock: 20, Ulrike Hammerich/Shutterstock: 21, Laurence Gough/Shutterstock: 22, Dobresum/ iStockphoto: 23,
NASA: 24, Elisei Shafer/Shutterstock: 25, Atanas.dk/ Shutterstock: 27, Peter Steiner/Alamy: 28, Agnieszka Ciura/Shutterstock: 29,
Serdar Yagci/iStockphoto: 30, David Maska/Shutterstock: 31, Dr. Morley Read/Shutterstock: 32, Eugene Hoshiko/Associated Press: 33,
Mike Hutchings/Reuters: 34, Norman Kin Hang Chan/123rf: 35, Flashon Studio/ Sutterstock: 36, Bill Ross/Corbis: 37,
Stephen Finn/Shutterstock: 38, Edwin Verin/Shutterstock: 39.
Q2AMedia Art Bank: 8, 10t, 10b, 12, 26, 41.

Printed in China

Franklin Watts is a division of Hachette Children's Books,
an Hachette UK company.
www.hachette.co.uk

CONTENTS

1

WHAT IS A CARBON FOOTPRINT?

A footprint is a mark that shows where someone has passed by. Every day, we leave an invisible mark on the planet – our carbon footprint – by releasing carbon gases.

Carbon gases

Since our ancestors discovered how to make fire hundreds of thousands of years ago, human activity has been changing the planet. And over the last 200 years, the rate of change has increased massively, affecting even the air around us. As people have begun to burn more coal, oil and gas, we have released increasing amounts of **carbon dioxide** (CO_2) into the air. Carbon gases, such as carbon dioxide and methane (CH_4), are the gases that make up our **carbon footprint**. We call them **carbon emissions.** Unfortunately, these gases are starting to have a serious effect on the planet.

Earth Data

- The level of CO_2 in the atmosphere today is higher than it has been at any time in the last 800,000 years.

- There is 37 per cent more CO_2 in the atmosphere now than there was 200 years ago.

- Before the modern age, the fastest known rise in CO_2 was 0.00003 per cent over 1,000 years. Between the 20th and 21st century, CO_2 levels rose that much in just 17 years.

Carbon gases absorb infrared radiation (heat) from the Sun, causing the planet to warm up.

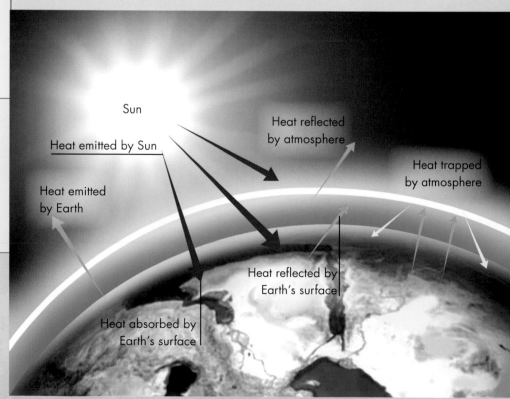

Sun

Heat emitted by Sun

Heat reflected by atmosphere

Heat trapped by atmosphere

Heat emitted by Earth

Heat reflected by Earth's surface

Heat absorbed by Earth's surface

As the balance of carbon gases in the atmosphere changes, some parts of the world are becoming too hot.

In the greenhouse

The Earth's atmosphere provides the air that we breathe. It is made up of a mixture of different gases. Some of these gases – called **greenhouse gases** – help to keep the planet warm. These gases absorb heat easily. The heat is then passed down to the ground, the sea and the rest of the air, warming the planet. We call this process 'the greenhouse effect' because the gases absorb heat (just as the air in a greenhouse gets very hot in the sunshine). Carbon dioxide and methane are both greenhouse gases.

The presence of greenhouse gases makes life on Earth possible. Without them, temperatures on our planet would vary widely between day and night – too hot and too cold for anything to survive. Some greenhouse gases are needed to absorb warmth from the Sun and to keep these temperatures safely balanced.

The right balance

The balance of greenhouse gases on Earth has been just right for the survival of human, animal and plant life on the planet for hundreds of thousands of years. Other planets have different balances of gases, and very different **climates**.

The planet Mercury has no atmosphere, so no greenhouse gases. The temperature on Mercury ranges between – 170°C and 350°C. The side of Mercury that faces away from the Sun loses all its heat to space immediately. In contrast, Venus has a thick atmosphere with a strong greenhouse effect. There, the temperature is a sizzling 464°C.

The Earth's atmosphere is just right – it keeps in enough heat from the Sun to stop the temperature plummeting at night, but not so much that we overheat. But in the modern world, with our reliance on fuels and factories, the atmosphere is changing and the warning signs are clear.

Carbon emissions

There are several different types of greenhouse gases. Carbon dioxide and methane are the most important and make up the carbon footprint. About 70 per cent of our carbon footprint is CO_2. To reduce this footprint, we need to cut the amount of carbon dioxide and methane that we release into the atmosphere.

Carbon dioxide is produced when fuels burn. This is the source of much of the extra CO_2 in the atmosphere today. But human activities are not the only cause of carbon gases. When humans, plants and animals **respire** (breathe) they produce CO_2. Decaying plants and animals also produce CO_2 and methane. This is part of the natural cycle of life on Earth. Wildfires and **volcanic** eruptions can also produce large amounts of CO_2. These natural events are not a problem – the problem comes from the extra carbon emissions we produce from industrialised activities.

Industrialisation

The level of CO_2 in the atmosphere has risen rapidly since the start of the **Industrial Revolution**, when people began to burn more fuels to run machinery and vehicles. Today, we burn more fuels than ever before and the level of CO_2 in the atmosphere is rising very quickly. With an increase in greenhouse gases, the temperature of the planet rises, too. Although temperatures on Earth have varied over millions of years, the rise over the last 200 years does not match any rise seen before in the history of mankind. Rising temperatures will have a dire effect on people around the world.

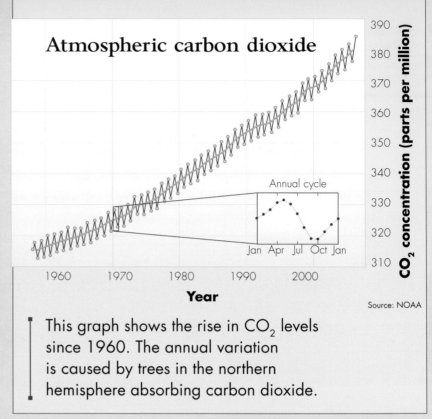

This graph shows the rise in CO_2 levels since 1960. The annual variation is caused by trees in the northern hemisphere absorbing carbon dioxide.

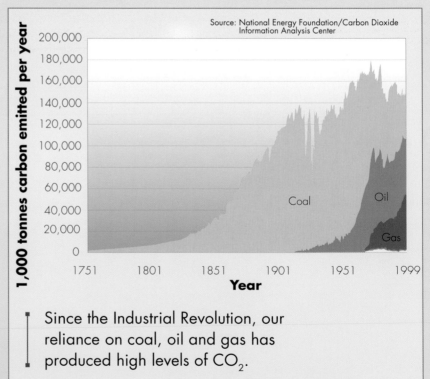

Since the Industrial Revolution, our reliance on coal, oil and gas has produced high levels of CO_2.

A recipe for disaster

As the population of the world has grown rapidly, and industrialisation has spread, the carbon footprint has become larger. Many scientists believe the current situation is not sustainable. They warn that the Earth will warm up, and other aspects of the climate will change, because of the build-up of greenhouse gases. As a result, patterns of life on Earth will change. The carbon footprint must be reduced quickly to avert disaster.

Uneven footprints

Scientists speak of the carbon footprint of the whole human race, but each person also has an individual carbon footprint. People with different lifestyles produce varying amounts of greenhouse gases, so have different carbon footprints.

In more economically developed countries (**MEDCs**), people use a lot of fuel to heat and cool buildings, power vehicles and run machinery. They have a large carbon footprint. In less economically developed countries (**LEDCs**), most people live much simpler lives. They often do not have heating or cooling systems, and if they have a vehicle it may be a bicycle or a vehicle pulled by an animal. They do not buy many manufactured goods or travel long distances. Their carbon footprint is much smaller.

PLANET WATCH

These greenhouse gases cause global warming:

» Carbon dioxide (CO_2)
» Methane (CH_4)
» Hydrofluorocarbons (HFCs)
» Perfluorocarbons (PFCs)
» Sulphur hexafluoride (SF)
» Nitrous oxide (N_2O)

Water vapour high in the atmosphere also acts as a greenhouse gas.

People in Uzbekistan who live in tents like these have a small carbon footprint.

2 FROM CARBON CYCLE TO VICIOUS CIRCLE

Normally, the Earth recycles carbon to keep CO_2 levels stable. But as carbon gases have increased, the delicate balance has shifted — and the consequences could be disastrous.

The carbon cycle

The amount of carbon on Earth is fixed, but it moves between different states constantly. Life on Earth depends on the carbon cycle that has developed over billions of years. The CO_2 produced by respiring and decaying plants and animals is removed by **carbon sinks**. Plants are a carbon sink: they take in CO_2 and release oxygen during **photosynthesis**. Some sea animals are carbon sinks – they build a shell or skeleton from calcium, carbon and oxygen. When they die, they are buried deep beneath the seabed. It is a long time before the carbon is released again.

Earth Data

- The carbon footprint must be reduced to an average of 2 tonnes of CO_2 per person each year to keep conditions stable.

- A person could use their carbon allowance of 2 tonnes by taking a single flight from London to Hong Kong, but then they would have none left for other travel, heating or using electrical appliances.

- Two tonnes is one fifth of the CO_2 used by a person in the UK, or one tenth of that used by a person in the USA.

The carbon dioxide cycle keeps a careful balance of carbon on Earth, but this natural cycle is changing.

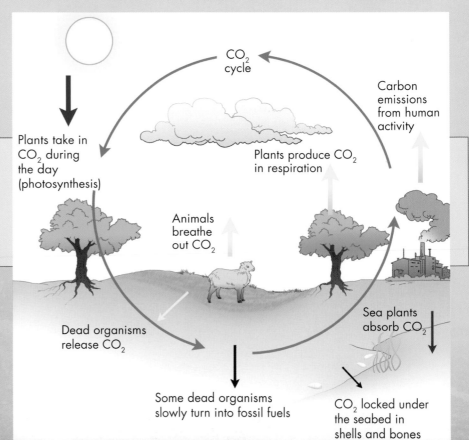

CO_2 cycle

Carbon emissions from human activity

Plants take in CO_2 during the day (photosynthesis)

Plants produce CO_2 in respiration

Animals breathe out CO_2

Dead organisms release CO_2

Sea plants absorb CO_2

Some dead organisms slowly turn into fossil fuels

CO_2 locked under the seabed in shells and bones

Fossil fuels and carbon

Fossil fuels are fuels such as coal, oil and gas. They are another type of carbon sink, and were produced over millions of years from organisms such as plants and plankton. The dead material has been squashed under pressure for a very long time, and **geological** processes have changed it into fossil fuels. When fossil fuels are burned, carbon which has been locked away for millions of years is released into the atmosphere.

Disturbing the cycle

Although human activity is responsible for only 3 per cent of the CO_2 produced each year, it is enough to disrupt the carefully balanced natural cycle. The planet cannot immediately absorb the extra CO_2 which has been released so suddenly after millions of years. This extra carbon has now built up in the atmosphere.

Energy and carbon

At present, 90 per cent of the energy we use comes from burning fossil fuels. We burn so much that some types of fossil fuels are likely to run out in our lifetime. Fossil fuels are used to move our vehicles, to run our power stations and to operate our heating systems.

Most power stations burn fossil fuels. This means that when you use electricity in your home, for example, CO_2 is added to the atmosphere. Activities such as using a computer, turning on the air conditioning, boiling a kettle, watching a DVD and heating water for a shower all increase the levels of carbon emissions.

We use fossils fuels in other ways, too. We rely on gas, oil or coal for our heating. Many people have gas cookers in their homes. **Petroleum**, from oil, helps to run our vehicles. Oil is also refined to make the plastic items that we use each day.

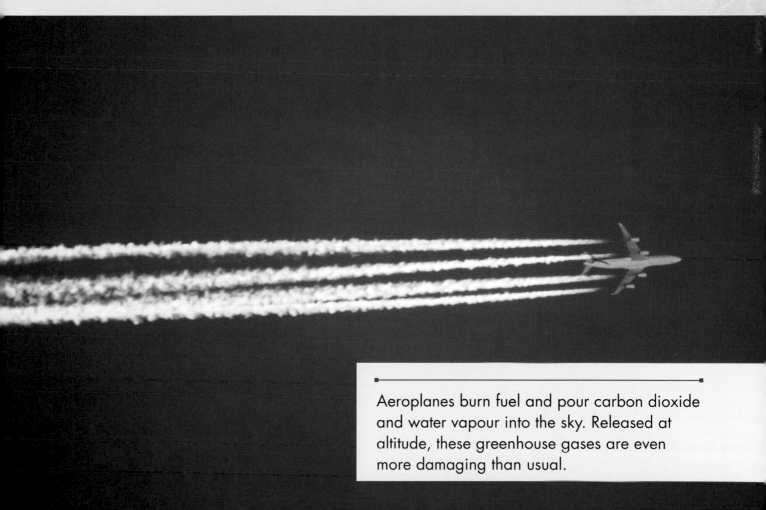

Aeroplanes burn fuel and pour carbon dioxide and water vapour into the sky. Released at altitude, these greenhouse gases are even more damaging than usual.

Carbon all around us

Industry and modern agriculture use a lot of energy. Manufactured goods, from clothing to furniture and electrical items, all have carbon footprints because energy has been used to make and to move them (see page 29). Even food has a considerable carbon footprint, because it has been tended, harvested and transported. Food that is processed – whether by being washed and cut up, or by being made into ready meals – produces even more carbon emissions.

Cutting down trees

At the same time as we add more CO_2 to the atmosphere by burning fossil fuels, we are also cutting down forests which absorb CO_2. People cut down forests to clear land for building and farming. Even when land is used for farming, the low-growing crops which replace the trees remove less CO_2 than the lush vegetation that covered the land as forest.

A hotter world

As CO_2 increases in the atmosphere, the greenhouse effect increases, too. Heat is not able to escape into space as easily, and the Earth warms up. As the world warms, weather patterns will continue to change and ice will melt more quickly. Over time, these changes will have a huge impact on people around the world. As the weather alters, plants and animals that live in a particular area will begin to change, too. Some pests and diseases will start to affect areas where they currently cannot survive. Future generations will have new problems to deal with.

These trees have been cut and burned to provide land for agriculture. There are now fewer trees in this forest to absorb carbon dioxide from the atmosphere.

Malaria is spread from the bite of mosquitoes carrying a tiny parasite. If weather patterns change, more areas will be at risk of insect-borne diseases.

PLANET WATCH

» The average temperature on Earth rose 0.7°C in the last century.

» At the current rate of rising carbon emissions, the temperature is set to rise another 0.5°C by 2025, and at least 2°C (though possibly as much as 6°C) by 2100.

» A rise of 2°C is enough to melt all small glaciers around the world, causing a shortage of drinking water in many areas.

» A rise of 4–6°C is enough to raise sea levels to threaten low-lying cities such as London, New York and Shanghai.

More water

The **ice-cap** near the North Pole is already melting quickly. A few years ago, scientists feared that the North Pole would be free of ice during the summer within 50 years. Now it is likely to happen within five or ten years. The ice at the North Pole floats on water – there is no land beneath it. As the sea warms up, this ice melts more quickly.

Glaciers around the world are also shrinking rapidly as they melt – a problem for people who depend on glaciers for their fresh water supply. When ice on land melts, the extra water runs into the ocean. This causes rising sea levels and a risk of flooding in coastal areas around the world. Already, the islands of Tuvalu in the Pacific are badly flooded at **surge tides**. The highest point on the islands is less than 5 metres above sea level. At surge tides, the sea rises 3 metres. Water seeps up through the ground, and the soil is already too salty to grow crops. In 2001, people from Tuvalu became the world's first **climate refugees**, moving to New Zealand because they were evacuated from their flooding islands.

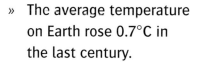

Ice cores are long cylinders of ice drilled from ice sheets. Bubbles trapped in the ice cores reveal how levels of methane and CO_2 in the atmosphere have changed over hundreds of thousands of years.

Ice under the land

The ice-caps and glaciers are not the only ice that is melting. **Permafrost** is a layer of frozen ground in Arctic regions. As the planet warms, the permafrost is melting. Water begins to replace the ice and the ground **subsides**. In areas such as northern Russia, Alaska and Scandinavia, the ground is no longer held solid by the permafrost – buildings and roads are sinking and pipelines are beginning to crack.

But the permafrost holds another, more serious danger. Deposits of **methane hydrate** are frozen within the permafrost. This is a frozen mixture of methane gas and water below ground and under the seabed, laid down thousands or millions of years ago. The melting permafrost will release billions of tonnes of methane into the atmosphere, a greenhouse gas 20 times more powerful than CO_2. This will make the greenhouse effect worse, causing more warming and more melting in a vicious circle. As a result, global temperatures are rising far faster than scientists first imagined. This type of effect – when the outcome of a change causes even more change to occur – is called a **positive feedback loop**.

16

Tipping point

In many systems, there is a **tipping point** – a point beyond which change speeds up rapidly. Scientists have suggested several tipping points that could cause **climate change** to spiral out of control. As temperatures on Earth increase, for example, more ice melts and sea levels rise. The dark sea absorbs much more heat from the Sun than pale, reflective ice. As a result, rising sea levels and shrinking ice cover will lead to further warming and melting.

Scientists first began to notice the rise in CO_2 in the atmosphere in the 1950s. For many years, very few people thought the change was important. In the 1990s, more people began to realise that the rise in CO_2 may be caused by human activity and linked to climate change. Even so, many others argued that the rising levels were just part of a natural cycle. Scientists are now in general agreement that human activity is to blame and further changes must be prevented.

What are we doing about it?

The first international effort to tackle the problem was the Kyoto Protocol, an agreement made in 1997 that came into force in 2005. Under the protocol, MEDCs agreed to reduce their carbon emissions and to help developing LEDCs keep their carbon emissions low. However, many nations are falling behind with their targets. Some countries, such as the USA, haven't fully approved the treaty. Others, such as India, are exempt while they develop.

PLANET WATCH

» The permafrost has been frozen since the last **Ice Age**, 11,000 years ago.

» The Siberian permafrost covers an area the size of France and Germany.

» Temperatures in western Siberia are rising faster than in many other places. The average temperature has gone up 3°C in the last 40 years.

» The permafrost locks in 70 billion tonnes of methane.

» Over 100 years, the annual output of escaped methane would be the same as the methane produced by agriculture and the world's wetlands each year, but the methane may escape in as little as 20 years.

The Pacific islands of Tuvalu will be lost to the sea for ever if sea levels continue to rise (see page 15).

3 ALTERNATIVE TECHNOLOGIES

To prevent catastrophic events, we must reduce our carbon footprint now. Many people hope that scientific solutions will provide an answer to our energy needs.

Energy for the future

Our lifestyles depend on producing and using a lot of energy, so it will not be possible to change that quickly. Instead, many scientists are trying to produce 'clean' energy from **renewable** resources. Clean energy produces little or no greenhouse gas emissions. Renewable resources are those that are naturally replenished, and are not used up. Fossil fuels are not a renewable resource because they take millions of years to form. Once we have used all the fossil fuels, there will be none for a very long time.

Every time we fill our cars with petrol or diesel we are using fossil fuels that have taken millions of years to form. These fuels cannot be replaced.

The solar cells in this outdoor light store energy from sunlight in a battery. The energy is used when it gets dark to power the lightbulb.

Energy efficiency

Developing sources of energy which are clean and renewable will take time. A good short-term solution is to make existing technologies more energy-efficient, so that they use less energy and produce lower levels of greenhouse gases.

Some technologies can be made more efficient by small changes. For example, a car will use less fuel if the tyres are fully inflated and the engine properly tuned. A car will also use less fuel if it is driven smoothly – accelerating and decelerating slowly – and if it does not carry unnecessary extra weight. Similarly, heating a building is more efficient if the building is well **insulated**, to prevent heat escaping to the air outside.

Some technologies can even make use of their own waste energy. A **hybrid car**, for example, stores the energy produced by braking and uses it to drive the vehicle. While the car is moving at low speeds, or stopping and starting frequently, this is very efficient. On longer journeys with little braking, however, the car has to use more petrol.

Biofuels

Biofuels are fuels made from plant matter, such as corn stalks, maize or sugar cane. Some animal waste, such as chicken droppings, can also be used to make biofuels. The process of making biofuels does not release as much greenhouse gas as preparing fossil fuels. When fossil fuels are burned, they release carbon that has been locked away for millions of years, but plants have only just absorbed the carbon in biofuels. This means that biofuels do not disrupt the carbon cycle.

Low-carbon energy

Although we can use technologies more efficiently, these activities still use fuels and they produce carbon emissions in the process. A better long-term solution is to use sources of energy that are **carbon-neutral** – these energy sources produce no increase in carbon emissions. There are plenty of options: we can get energy from the Sun, wind, water and below the ground, for example. We can also use nuclear power and **hydrogen cells**.

Energy from the Sun

Energy from the Sun has fallen on the Earth for billions of years. The Sun's energy has enabled plants and animals to grow. Enough **solar energy** falls on to the Earth every minute to fulfil our energy needs for a whole year. So why don't we harness more of this energy and use it? Solar power is free, permanently renewed and completely clean. But it is not equally available everywhere – some places are exposed to more Sun than others. Sunlight is also only available during the day.

Simple technology

Solar power can be used actively or passively. Buildings designed to make the best possible use of the sunlight that falls on them are using **passive solar power**. Such buildings have windows to let in natural light and use building materials that absorb and store warmth from the Sun, releasing it later as a form of heating.

Active solar power needs extra technologies to convert or store heat or light from the Sun. Solar panels on a building, for example, use **photovoltaic cells** to generate electricity. Another type of solar panel contains liquid that is heated by the Sun. The heat is used to warm water for washing or heating, or to warm the building's concrete blocks. A solar power station also generates electricity from the Sun's energy. Energy is needed to build the power station, but once in place it has a minimal carbon footprint.

The photovoltaic cells on this building convert the Sun's radiation into electricity that can be used to power appliances inside.

At present, photovoltaic cells are expensive to make and are not very efficient – little of the energy from the Sun that falls on a cell is converted to electricity. But scientists are working to improve this technology. Flexible solar panels are also being developed – these are easy to carry around and can be draped over irregularly shaped objects to catch sunlight wherever they can.

Wind power

Wind has also been used as a source of energy for hundreds of years. It has been used to power boats and to drive windmills which grind corn.

Modern wind **turbines** use a generator to convert movement (produced by the energy of the wind) into electricity. The electricity can be used locally or fed into the national grid.

To make the most of wind power, turbines are put on hills, in exposed areas, or offshore in the sea. They are often grouped together in wind farms. Where there are few obstacles to stop the strength of the wind, the turbines can generate a lot of power. Wind turbines on land are not always popular, however. Some people object to the noise they make and think they are ugly. They can also be dangerous to birds that fly in their path.

With fossil fuels on the decline, wind farms like this will become a more popular source of energy.

PLANET WATCH

» Large solar power stations are being built in parts of the world that receive a lot of sunlight, such as Australia, parts of the USA and the Middle East.

» Some of the places most likely to be affected by climate change are also those that can easily use solar power.

» The process of manufacturing solar panels produces carbon emissions. It therefore takes several years to earn back enough energy for this type of power to be carbon-neutral.

Power from water

Flowing rivers and ocean tides are another potential source of energy. Watermills use a river's rushing water to drive a wheel. In the past, watermills were used to grind corn or to carry out other tasks that required a turning mechanism. But water power can also be used to generate electricity. **Hydroelectric power** stations use running water to drive a turbine linked to a generator. Around a fifth of the world's electricity is already provided by hydroelectric power stations. Although new power stations are expensive to build, and carbon emissions are produced during this process, they are eventually cheap to run and produce no polluting gases.

Geothermal energy

Not all the Earth's heat comes from the Sun; a good proportion is generated deep within the Earth, at the super-heated **core**. The temperature of the Earth's core is 6,000–7,000°C. By drilling down a few metres into the ground, it is possible to draw off some of this heat. In some parts of the world, naturally occurring hot springs bring this **geothermal** heat to the surface. In Iceland, for example, the semi-molten layer of the Earth's **mantle** is very close to the Earth's surface (or **crust**). In some places, semi-molten rock from the mantle actually breaks through the Earth's surface. We call this volcanic activity.

Geothermal energy can be used to provide hot water for homes – water pipes can be passed through hot rocks, or cold water pumped underground to absorb the heat. On a larger scale, geothermal power stations draw on the Earth's constant supply of internal heat to produce steam to drive turbines. Some geothermal power stations produce carbon emissions, but even then, the level is much lower (about a twentieth) of the emissions produced by fossil fuel power stations. The gases produced are also often pumped back into the Earth, burying them underground rather than letting them escape into the atmosphere. This is not dangerous – the gases are simply going back to where they came from.

This geothermal power station in Iceland uses the Earth's heat to generate electricity.

Nuclear power

Nuclear power stations produce power from the energy within **atoms**, the tiny particles that make up matter. At present, the **nuclear reactors** at these power stations are fission reactors, which break atoms apart to release energy. In the future, nuclear fusion reactors may produce energy by forcing atoms together. The first fusion reactor is planned for Cadarache, France, for 2018. The European Union (EU), China, Japan, India, South Korea, Russia and the USA are involved in this international project.

Accidents at nuclear power stations can have devastating effects. Nuclear power stations have to be carefully managed and security is tight. The waste that is produced also remains radioactive for thousands of years. It has to be stored safely in special cooling ponds or buried underground. Nuclear reactors are expensive and time-consuming to build, so they are not a short-term solution to the energy problem. However, once made, they are cheap to run and, despite the dangers, offer a way of generating energy without producing polluting carbon gases.

> Nuclear power stations currently generate about a fifth of the world's electricity, but we may need to rely on them even more in the future.

PLANET WATCH

» In 2005, 88 per cent of all electricity from the world's renewable sources came from hydroelectric power.

» China has over half of the world's small hydroelectric installations.

» A study by the Massachusetts Institute of Technology worked out that there is enough heat energy in rocks 10 km below the surface of the USA to provide all the world's power needs for 30,000 years.

Hydrogen cells

Hydrogen cells also use energy from atoms, but instead of using the energy within atoms to generate electricity, they use the spare energy produced by a chemical reaction. A hydrogen cell works in a way that is similar to an ordinary battery. Hydrogen and oxygen combine in the cell to form water, releasing energy in the process. There are no carbon emissions – water is the only waste product.

Hydrogen can also be burned to drive cars and buses without releasing the CO_2 that fossil fuels produce. Hydrogen is very light and can be stored in the vehicle. It is then mixed with oxygen from the air to generate heat and electricity to power the engine. The most common source of hydrogen is water, so this energy source is certainly plentiful. However, separating the hydrogen from water is a very expensive process. It also uses electricity, thereby producing carbon emissions.

Hydrogen would be an ideal fuel for spacecraft. Small amounts of this light gas can power a very long journey.

Carbon in the near future

It will take a long time for the world to start producing all its energy from renewable, carbon-neutral sources. At the moment, scientists and politicians are still debating the best methods of providing energy for the future. Even when a decision is made, it takes time to fund and build new power stations or equipment, and put them into use.

While electrical goods will run equally well whatever the source of the electricity, the same is not true of items that use other sources of energy. A vehicle that has been built to use petrol or diesel cannot run solely on biofuels or hydrogen without being adapted. A house heated by gas would need completely different equipment if it were to be

24

heated by solar power. Whatever decisions we reach about future energy sources, we will still produce carbon emissions in the meantime while vehicles and buildings are being modified.

Locking it away

To prevent the extra CO_2 adding to the damage which has already been done, it can be **sequestered** – locked away – where it cannot escape into the atmosphere. There are several ways of doing this. One is to use natural organisms to **metabolise** the carbon. Planting trees is an example – since trees absorb carbon – but there is limited land available to plant more trees. The sea offers more scope for locking carbon away. Salps are small sea creatures that can take in carbon and expel it as pellets that sink to the bottom of the sea. The carbon will lie there for many years before it escapes again. Seaweed farms are another way to absorb carbon at sea. Experimental seaweed farms near Japan grow great rafts of fast-growing seaweed that absorb CO_2. The seaweed can also be converted to biofuels.

We can dump carbon deposits deep underground, too, where they will lie buried for a long time. Already, some exhausted oil mines are used for dumping carbon. By locking carbon underground, we put the carbon released from fossil fuels back where it came from.

PLANET WATCH

Electricity produced in the USA:

» 49.7 per cent from coal.

» 19.3 per cent from nuclear power.

» 18.7 per cent from natural gas.

» 6.5 per cent from hydroelectricity.

» 3 per cent from petroleum.

» 2.8 per cent from other sources.

These salps are absorbing carbon as they drift through the ocean. Their waste and remains will sink to the seabed where the carbon will be buried and locked away.

4 CHANGING LIFESTYLES

Every person has a carbon footprint. Whether your impact is large or small, reducing carbon emissions is an important challenge facing us all.

A personal footprint

A carbon footprint is usually measured as the mass of CO_2 produced each year. To live sustainably in the world, scientists have calculated that each person's carbon footprint needs to be no more than 2 tonnes of CO_2 each year. That means a person in the UK must cut their carbon footprint by 80 per cent and a person in the USA must cut it by 90 per cent. It will take considerable change on the part of both individuals and governments to achieve that.

Carbon footprints around the world

People in different societies have very different carbon footprints. In MEDCs, most people have a carbon footprint much larger than 2 tonnes. Our energy-hungry modern lifestyles depend on using fuel for everything. People have their own cars, buy goods that have been imported or made in factories, and expect to keep their buildings at an even temperature throughout the year.

This map shows the amount of carbon produced per person in the different countries of the world each year.

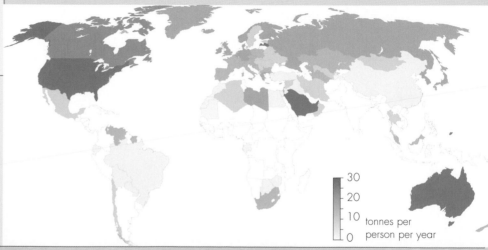

30
20
10
0

tonnes per person per year

Source: US Department of Energy's Carbon Dioxide Information Analysis Center (CDIAC)

26

In contrast, people in LEDCs have few possessions they have not made themselves or bought locally. Their homes are unheated and uncooled; they often have no electricity or vehicles to get around. Their food is grown locally and is not processed in factories. Their carbon footprint is very small.

Is it fair?

The people who are responsible for the carbon footprint are not those who will suffer most from its effects. Some people in Africa and Asia, many of whom have a very low carbon footprint, are already short of water and cannot grow food on their land. Others find their communities are flooded by rising sea levels. These communities will not be able to improve their situation unless MEDCs start to take responsibility for carbon emissions, too. A fair solution will involve making sure that people in LEDCs can improve their standard of living without suffering the effects of climate change, while people in MEDCs cut back their emissions.

> City life is powered by a huge amount of energy, from heating and lighting buildings to transport, services and entertainment.

Your carbon footprint

We need to consider where our carbon footprint comes from, to reduce it effectively. Each person produces carbon emissions both directly and indirectly. We call these **primary** (or direct) **emissions** and **secondary** (or indirect) **emissions**. Primary emissions come from energy we use directly ourselves – from the fuels we burn, and from the electricity we use to power things. They come from heating and lighting our homes, our transport needs, and the electrical items we use. Secondary emissions are harder to measure. They come from energy that has been used on our behalf. They include the fuel and electricity used to make and move everything we buy.

This rickshaw is a useful way to get around the city – and unlike a conventional taxi, it produces no carbon emissions.

Active and passive emissions

Individual carbon footprints can also be divided into **active** and **passive emissions**. Active emissions are carbon gases produced directly by an individual's activities, such as flying abroad on holiday, heating a home and buying consumer goods. Passive emissions are carbon gases produced by the society the person lives in, and over which he or she has no direct control. Examples are street lighting, running government buildings and maintaining an army. Individuals cannot immediately reduce their passive emissions, but they can campaign or vote for change to encourage governments to act.

First things first

People can take three types of action to reduce their primary emissions: avoid wasting energy, use energy more efficiently, and use less energy. Our lifestyles don't have to change dramatically to avoid wasting energy. Switching off lights in empty rooms, turning off chargers or items left on standby, and turning the heating off when everyone is out are a few examples.

Insulating homes so that heat does not escape can cut energy used on heating by a third. Using energy efficiently takes a little thought, but is easy to achieve. It means using a washing machine only when it is full, or combining trips and sharing lifts to reduce car use. It means choosing more energy-efficient items or options, such as heating water for a quick shower instead of a deep bath.

Using less energy needs a greater change in lifestyle. It involves turning the heating down and putting on a thicker jumper instead, walking or cycling short distances instead of driving, drying clothes outside instead of in a dryer, and giving up or cutting down on flights abroad. It will be more difficult for people to change these habits.

Hidden carbon

Passive emissions are hidden in everything we buy. When we buy food from a supermarket, or clothes from a shop, those items have their own carbon footprint.

The food was grown by a farmer who used fuel to power his tractors (and perhaps to heat greenhouses). The farmer also used tools and perhaps fertilisers with their own carbon footprint. The food was then transported, and perhaps processed and packed, using more fuel.

Every manufactured item also has a carbon footprint. Many products are wrapped in packaging that has taken energy to produce and is quickly thrown away.

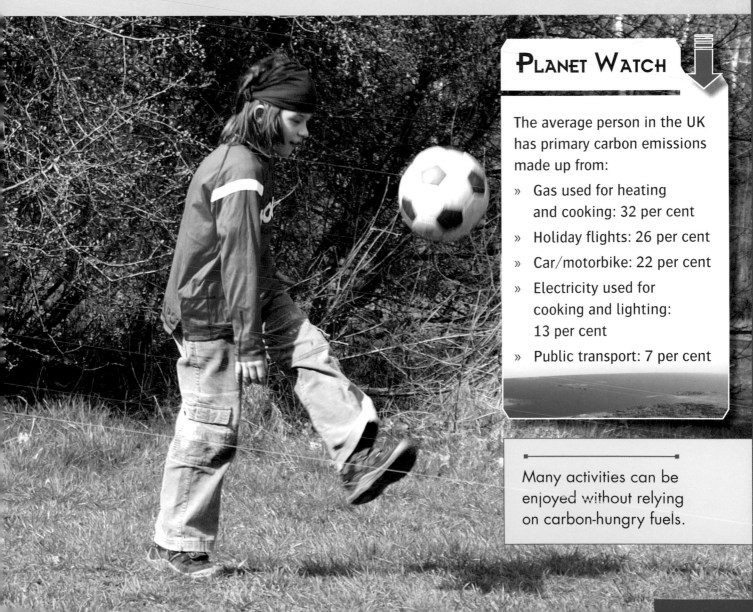

PLANET WATCH

The average person in the UK has primary carbon emissions made up from:

» Gas used for heating and cooking: 32 per cent

» Holiday flights: 26 per cent

» Car/motorbike: 22 per cent

» Electricity used for cooking and lighting: 13 per cent

» Public transport: 7 per cent

Many activities can be enjoyed without relying on carbon-hungry fuels.

Life Cycle Assessment

Life Cycle Assessment (LCA) is a way of measuring the carbon impact of manufactured goods. It looks at a product's whole 'life'. For a glass bottle, for example, it would begin with the energy used to extract the minerals used to make the glass and end when the bottle can no longer be re-used (including the carbon emissions produced by disposing of it). It is a complicated calculation.

LCA figures can help us to take responsibility for our secondary carbon emissions. They help people to choose more energy-efficient options. Some products are now labelled with LCA carbon figures. A packet of crisps may show it has a carbon footprint of 75 grams of carbon, for example. But labelling is not yet compulsory.

Farming and food

We all have to eat – but some food choices are more carbon-hungry than others. Meat is the least carbon-efficient food. Land is used to keep animals and to grow the food that feeds them. And the process is inefficient: it takes 700 calories of animal feed to produce 100 calories of beef, for example. Animal waste also produces methane, a powerful greenhouse gas.

A huge amount of energy is used to grow and move food. In wealthy societies, people have become used to eating meat, to having fruit and vegetables out of season, or foods from other countries. Some food is flown around the world, or grown in heated greenhouses, giving the food a very large carbon footprint.

Our shops are filled with goods, such as fruit and vegetables, which have been imported from abroad.

Every year worldwide, we throw away around 20–50 million tonnes of electrical waste.

PLANET WATCH

» Nearly a fifth of all greenhouse gas emissions come from producing and transporting meat and dairy products – more than from all transport.

» The most energy-efficient animal protein is a farmed fish called tilapia. It takes 1.7 kg of feed to produce 1 kg of tilapia.

» Producing 1 kg of beef produces as much CO_2 as leaving a 100-watt light bulb on for nearly 20 days and nights, or driving a European car 250 km.

» The ingredients of a traditional Christmas dinner in the UK (like a Thanksgiving meal in the USA) may have been flown a total of 10,000 km or more.

Lean and efficient

In wealthy societies, people buy far more than they need. It is usual for people to have more than one television, more than one computer, and lots of clothes and shoes. Most people throw away anything that is broken or tired-looking. They may throw away clothes just because they are no longer fashionable. Around a third of the food we buy is wasted – either because it is left on the plate and thrown away, or because it is kept until past its use-by date and then thrown out. We all need to learn to buy only what we need, waste less, and recycle anything we no longer want or use.

5 TRADING AND OFFSETTING

In the modern world, it is not easy to change people's attitudes and use of energy. One way to help the transition is to give rewards and incentives for reducing carbon emissions.

Setting limits

An effective way to start reducing the carbon footprint is to limit the amount of carbon an individual, organisation or country can produce. The Kyoto Protocol, agreed to in 1997, has set targets for many countries to cut their carbon emissions by 2012. Countries may use whatever measures they choose to meet their targets. Some developing countries are allowed to increase their carbon emissions, but within limits. Unfortunately, not all developed countries have agreed to make the needed cuts. China, which produces more carbon emissions than any other country, will join in at the next round (after 2012) – as long as the USA has begun to cut emissions, too.

Earth Data

- Under the Kyoto Protocol, the USA agreed to cut carbon emissions to 6 per cent less than their 1990 level, but then they pulled out. In 2008, US emissions had risen more than 15 per cent since 1990.

- Estimates show that India's emissions may have risen by as much as 50 per cent since 1990. But India is not required to cut emissions under the current terms of the Kyoto Protocol.

Many countries have decided to grow more forests to help meet their targets for reducing carbon emissions.

These toys are made in China for export to other countries. Who should be responsible for the energy used in their manufacture?

Offsetting emissions

Under the Kyoto Protocol, a country can balance some emissions it produces by supporting projects that reduce levels of CO_2. This is called **carbon offsetting**. For example, planting a forest will reduce a country's carbon footprint because the trees in the forest absorb CO_2 while they are growing. MEDCs can also claim credit for helping to reduce emissions in the developing world.

Trading in carbon

Countries can trade their carbon allowance under the Kyoto agreement. If one country cannot achieve the cuts it has agreed to, it can buy credit from a country that does not need all of its own allowance. This is called **carbon trading**. Russia's emissions, for example, have dropped to 35 per cent below their level in 1990 because of the poor state of the Russian economy. This leaves Russia able to trade its carbon allowance. The Russian government has said that it will use any income from trading to build power stations that use renewable sources of energy.

Whose carbon is it anyway?

In 2006, China overtook the USA as the largest producer of carbon emissions. But this is not just because Chinese people are living more carbon-hungry lifestyles. China has been developing rapidly and has seen a marked improvement in standards of living. Individual carbon footprints have certainly increased, but the average Chinese person still has a carbon footprint less than a fifth of that of the average American. China's population is four times that of the USA and this makes the carbon footprint of China large even while the carbon footprint of each individual person is quite small.

China has increased its manufacturing industry and produces goods for the rest of the world. So is it fair to count this carbon produced as China's responsibility? Most of the goods are sold into western countries, and without the demand from the west they would not be produced. When we talk about an individual country's carbon footprint, we need to consider that the relationship between countries is extremely complex.

Public attitudes are changing. These people are protesting at government inaction against climate change at an international meeting.

Carbon trading for businesses

Carbon allowances and trading are already used within the countries of the EU. The EU Emissions Trading Scheme (ETS), for example, was introduced in 2005 to control carbon emissions from heavy industries, such as iron **smelting** and concrete manufacture, as well as emissions from power stations. These energy-intensive industries have been given a carbon allowance to use over a fixed period (such as 2008–2012). If an industry needs more than its allowance it can buy 'credit' from an industry that does not need its full allowance. The scheme covers 12,000 sites spread throughout the EU. It is a compulsory system – businesses cannot opt out of it.

There are also some voluntary carbon trading systems for businesses elsewhere, including the Chicago Climate Exchange in the USA. Organisations that take part are committed to reducing carbon emissions. Although the US government has not fully approved the Kyoto Protocol, many US states are introducing their own local measures to cut carbon emissions. In the UK, too, a voluntary scheme run by the Department for Environment,

Food and Rural Affairs (Defra) pays rewards to companies that cut their emissions. As climate change is becoming more critical, attitudes are shifting and many companies now want to be seen as carbon-friendly, to attract customers. Businesses are also realising that – at a time when oil prices are rising – energy-saving measures will also help them to cut considerable costs in the long-term.

Personal carbon allowances

In the future, some governments may choose to tackle the problem by giving each individual a personal carbon allowance. Filling a car with fuel, booking a train ticket or buying a television would use up part of this allowance. Individuals would not be allowed to use more than their carbon allowance without buying more carbon 'credit' from someone else. This would mean that people who want to drive a large car and fly abroad on holiday can pay to do so; and people who do without a car or live a low-carbon lifestyle can be rewarded. Countries could also encourage people to cut their carbon emissions by giving them money towards energy-saving equipment for their homes. Some countries already give grants to individuals to fit solar panels, wind turbines or insulation, for example.

Individual offsetting

Individuals can offset all or some of their carbon, too. An individual can pay to help projects that reduce carbon emissions elsewhere, or projects that absorb carbon. The money may go towards developing alternative energy sources, planting and maintaining forests or installing energy-saving technologies, for example.

Although offsetting carbon emissions is better than ignoring them, it is not as good as avoiding them in the first place. But it is a useful short-term measure, while the world makes the transition to low-carbon living.

Recycling the materials we use is a simple way to reduce carbon emissions.

塑膠物料 **Plastic Materials**

鋁罐 **Aluminium Cans**

廢紙 **Waste Paper**

PLANET WATCH

» The EU Emissions Trading Scheme covers half the carbon emissions of the EU and is the largest international carbon trading scheme in the world.

» New York State, USA, has a carbon emissions trading scheme aimed at cutting carbon emissions from electricity generation by 10 per cent from January 2009 to 2018.

» The Australian Carbon Trading Scheme is due to be launched in 2010.

TAKING THE LEAD

Reducing the carbon footprint is a challenge facing the whole world. Individuals, businesses and governments must all play a part. But who should make the first move?

Earth Data

- In the Republic of Ireland, customers pay a tax of 0.15 euros for plastic carrier bags. As a result, bag use has dropped by 90 per cent. Free plastic bags are banned completely in China, and the manufacture of very thin plastic bags is illegal there.

- The international chain of Marks and Spencer shops aims to be entirely carbon-neutral by 2012.

- The island of Samsø in Denmark is the largest carbon-neutral community in the world. It has a population of 4,200 people.

Airport passengers wait to check-in. Their flights will produce high carbon emissions, but some airlines now offer carbon offsetting as an option.

Who starts?

Everyone is responsible for their personal carbon footprint, and must look at ways of reducing it. It is easy for each person to reduce their primary carbon emissions. The actions of local and national governments, large corporations, and international organisations must then reduce secondary emissions.

As the importance of reducing the carbon footprint has become more obvious, people in many countries are looking to their governments and industry to help tackle the task.

Eurostar carries passengers between the UK and parts of Europe. This service is now carbon-neutral and attracts customers who are environmentally aware.

Looking after the world

International effort is needed to reduce the world's carbon footprint. It is difficult to get international agreement on what must be done, and in many countries governments are reluctant to take actions that will be unpopular with their people.

For a long time, the USA has refused to take part in international measures to reduce carbon emissions. The American people rely heavily on fossil fuels, particularly oil, and their lifestyles will have to change considerably if oil use is reduced. US leaders have tried to use science and technology to solve the problem, keeping American lifestyles intact. Many other countries have been happy to take immediate action to reduce emissions, at the same time as looking to technology to help in the future. But no country is reducing its carbon footprint sufficiently at the moment.

Good for business

Businesses that can show they are working to protect the planet – and reduce the carbon footprint of the goods and services they sell – are finding that they attract more customers. *Eurostar*, for example, is a high-speed train link between London and Paris, passing under the English Channel. Since late 2007, it has been carbon-neutral. Many passengers choose *Eurostar* over flights or ferries because they are making a choice that is less damaging to the environment.

It is becoming socially unacceptable, in some areas, to drive large fuel-hungry cars because they are bad for the environment. Car manufacturers are beginning to find that they can boost sales by stressing their 'green' (environment-friendly) features. If a business is to survive, it has to respond to the wishes of its customers.

Ruling from above

In some areas, governments must take the lead, with legislation. In Europe, for example, fuel companies selling fuel for vehicles will have to include 5 per cent fuel from renewable sources by 2010. This change has been imposed by governments; fuel companies would otherwise be reluctant to make the expensive adjustments.

Governments can also influence behaviour by taxing high-carbon products, such as long flights or fuel-guzzling cars, or by charging for road use. In London, UK, drivers in the city centre have to pay a congestion charge (fee). These types of measures help to reduce fuel consumption because many people would prefer to spend less money on fuel or road charges. Governments can also give grants to encourage people to use renewable energy sources or to improve energy efficiency. In Germany, the government gives grants to encourage the use of renewable energy sources such as solar power. Although it can be costly and disruptive for an individual to modify their home to make it energy-efficient, government grants are making the changes affordable and worthwhile.

Government schemes such as the congestion zone in London, UK, are helping to reduce carbon emissions from traffic in city centres.

Action from the ground up

It takes a long time for governments to put laws in place. In the meantime, there are many choices that individuals can make to reduce their carbon footprints before new laws come into force.

In our homes, we can make sure energy is used efficiently by insulating effectively to reduce heat loss. We can all turn off electrical items that are not being used. We can adjust our clothing rather than keeping the house at the same temperature all year. We can choose energy-efficient appliances and rechargeable batteries. Some people may also be able to install and use solar or wind power for some of their energy needs.

Congestion charging
C
Central ZONE
Mon - Fri
7 am - 6.30 pm

The future of our planet is in our hands. We all need to act together before it is too late.

In all areas of our lives, we can choose to consume less. We can buy fewer new items, and recycle or re-use as much as possible. We can choose public transport over private cars, and reduce the number of flights that we take. We can use our leisure time in activities that have a low (or zero) carbon footprint. We can choose the items we buy carefully, looking for those with a lower carbon footprint and buying from companies with a good record on environmental issues. All these are small, simple changes, but if we all do it, we can make a difference.

Too late?

Many scientists believe that we still have time to prevent serious climate change, but stress that we all need to make a difference. If we ignore the problem, the increasing carbon footprint will lead to catastrophic climate change, with people around the world losing their homes and livelihoods. To avert disaster, we must all act now.

PLANET WATCH

» To avoid catastrophic climate change, scientists predict the rise in global temperatures since 1800 should not exceed 2°C.

» Due to greenhouse gases already released, a rise of 1.3°C cannot be avoided.

» To keep the rise below 2°C, CO_2 levels in the atmosphere must stabilise at around 400 parts per million (ppm). The current level is about 387 ppm (rising 2ppm every year).

FACTS AND RECORDS

Key dates

1820s: The Industrial Revolution, with its dependence on fossil fuels, begins to have an impact on CO_2 concentrations in the atmosphere.

1850s: End of the Little Ice Age, a period of cooler weather which began c.1250. Glaciers began to shrink from around 1850.

1950s: Post-war industry causes the rise in CO_2 levels to accelerate quickly.

1958: Continuous monitoring of CO_2 in the atmosphere begins. First report that CO_2 levels are rising.

1988: International Panel on Climate Change created to provide independent information to governments and scientists working on climate change and carbon emissions.

1992: At the Earth Summit in Rio de Janeiro, many of the world's countries signed an agreement to develop a framework to limit carbon emissions to levels that would not interfere dangerously with the climate.

1997: Kyoto Protocol drawn up.

2002: The rise in CO_2 in the atmosphere during a single year goes above 2 parts per million (ppm) for the first time.

2005: Kyoto Protocol comes into force.

2005: Sudden large reduction in glaciers in Greenland, spilling water into the sea and contributing to rising sea levels.

2006: China's carbon emissions overtake those of the USA, making it the largest emitter of CO_2 in the world.

2012: Kyoto Protocol end date, when all targets should be met.

Carbon footprints around the world

Ranking	Country	Tonnes CO$_2$ per person, 2004
1	Qatar	69.2
2	Kuwait	38.0
10	United States	20.4
11	Canada	20.0
12	Norway	19.01
13	Australia	16.3
18	Saudi Arabia	13.4
29	Israel	10.8
30	Russia	10.5
32	Ireland	10.4
34	Japan	9.83
37	United Kingdom	9.79
38	Germany	9.79
41	South Africa	9.2
49	Poland	8.0
50	New Zealand	7.8
52	Italy	7.69
61	Iran	6.31
63	France	6.2
72	Hong Kong	5.36
89	Chile	3.87
91	China	3.84
95	North Korea	3.36
98	Turkey	3.14
101	Iraq	2.97
109	Cuba	2.30
113	Egypt	2.21
120	Brazil	1.80
133	India	1.20
135	Vietnam	1.18

Household energy consumption

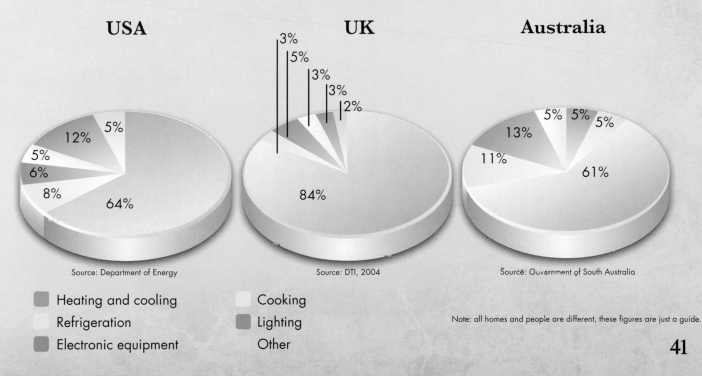

USA

Source: Department of Energy

UK

3%
5%
3%
3%
2%
84%

Source: DTI, 2004

Australia

5% 5% 5%
13%
11%
61%

Source: Government of South Australia

- Heating and cooling
- Refrigeration
- Electronic equipment
- Cooking
- Lighting
- Other

Note: all homes and people are different, these figures are just a guide.

41

GLOSSARY

active emissions
emissions produced by an individual's activities

active solar power
power converted from the Sun's heat or light to another type of energy

atom
a basic building block of matter

biofuel
a fuel made from biological materials, such as plant matter or animal waste

carbon dioxide
an atmospheric gas made up of carbon and oxygen

carbon emissions
gases containing carbon, released when a fuel is burned, for example

carbon footprint
a measure of the quantity of carbon emissions produced

carbon-neutral
producing no increase in carbon emissions

carbon offsetting
funding an activity which removes carbon or prevents greenhouse gases, to balance carbon use

carbon sink
something which absorbs carbon for a long time

carbon trading
a system of credits for carbon emissions which nations, organisations or individuals can trade

climate
the average weather of a region over a period of many years

climate change
a change in the temperature and weather systems of the world

climate refugees
people who have to leave their homes because climate change has made it impossible to stay in the area

core
the very centre of the Earth

crust
the thin, upper surface of the Earth which holds the landmasses and oceans

fossil fuel
a fuel derived from fossilised plant or animal remains

geological
relating to the processes which form and transform the rocks of the Earth

geothermal
relating to heat energy from deep within the Earth

glacier
a slow-moving mass of ice

greenhouse gases
gases which absorb heat easily and help to keep heat trapped near the Earth

hybrid car
a car which uses two sources of power, usually a fossil fuel (petrol or diesel) and a battery charged while the car is running

hydroelectric power
electricity generated from the movement of water

hydrogen cell
a device like a battery which produces electrical power from the chemical reaction of hydrogen and oxygen to produce water

Ice Age
the period when ice extends a long way south of the North Pole, covering much of Europe, and temperatures remain low for thousands of years

ice-cap
a layer of ice over the sea or land at the poles

Industrial Revolution
a period of sudden, rapid expansion of mechanised industries and growth of towns starting in the late 18th century

insulated
protected to prevent the transfer of heat

LEDCs
short for less economically developed countries, or the poorer countries of the world

mantle
the thick layer beneath the Earth's crust and above the core; composed of molten rock at a very high temperature

MEDCs
short for more economically developed countries, or the richer countries of the world

metabolise
to break down substances to produce energy

methane hydrate
a methane compound which exists in a frozen, solid form held in water ice

nuclear reactor
a device in which the energy from a nuclear reaction is used to generate electricity

passive emissions
emissions produced by the activities of a whole society

passive solar power
the energy from the Sun used without complex equipment

permafrost
a layer of permanently frozen ground beneath the surface

petroleum
a type of refined oil

photosynthesis
the process carried out by green plants that involves taking in CO_2 and releasing oxygen

photovoltaic cell
a device which produces electricity from solar energy

positive feedback loop
the system in which the results of a process feed back in to the process, keeping it going

primary emissions
carbon emissions produced by a person's direct use of fuels

renewable
able to be replenished

respire
breathe, taking oxygen from the air to use in the body and breathing out CO_2

secondary emissions
the carbon emissions produced in the manufacture of goods

sequester
to set apart

smelting
producing pure metal from a metal ore

solar energy
energy coming from the Sun or made by using the Sun's energy

subside
to give way

surge tide
the tide which brings water further in land, or to a greater depth, than usual, often resulting from a storm

tipping point
a point after which change will be very rapid

turbine
a mechanism which generates electricity by its turning action

volcanic
relating to the action of volcanoes, which bring semi-molten rock from deep within the Earth to the surface

FURTHER READING

- *An Inconvenient Truth: The Crisis of Global Warming (Young Adult edition)*, by Al Gore (Bloomsbury 2007)
- *How to Reduce Your Carbon Footprint: 365 Simple Ways…* by Joanna Yarrow (Chronicle Books, 2008)
- *i-Count: Your Step-by-Step Guide to Climate Bliss*, by Rob Alcraft (Penguin 2006)
- *Is Our Climate Changing? (Global Questions)* by Anne Rooney (Franklin Watts, 2008)

INDEX

WEBFINDER

http://news.bbc.co.uk/1/hi/sci/tech/5314592.stm
The ice core record of the world's changing carbon footprint
www.bbc.co.uk/climate/evidence/greenhouse_effect_img5.shtml
An animation showing how the greenhouse effect works
www.foe.co.uk/campaigns/climate/issues/climate_change/index.html
An explanation of the causes of climate change
www.sciencemuseum.org.uk/antenna/climatechange/
A guide to climate change and how the world is likely to change over the next 40 years
www.esrl.noaa.gov/gmd/ccgg/trends/
The latest world CO_2 figures and how the carbon footprint is changing, updated monthly
http://actonco2.direct.gov.uk/index.html
Calculate your carbon footprint